The Journey of a Bald Eagle Family
In the Hudson Valley

written and illustrated by

Debbie Quick

ISBN-13: 978-0692283356

DEDICATION

For my nieces and nephews: Mariah, Branden, Julia, Emily, Tyler, Kayla and Sophia. I look forward to teaching you all everything I know about bald eagles.

I love all of you very much!

The Journey of a Bald Eagle Family
In the Hudson Valley

Presented to:

_____

By:

_____

Date:

_____

Nestled high in a tulip tree close to the Hudson River lies a very big nest where new members of the Bald Eagle family arrive. The Mama and Papa eagles created the nest many years ago and every year they use it for their new babies.

In January, the Mama and Papa eagles start to bring sticks and grass to the nest. They use these items to raise the walls of the nest higher and higher to get it ready for the new babies they hope to have.

Once the walls of the nest are the right height for a family of eagles, the Mama eagle lays her eggs. Because it's cold out, one of the adult eagles must sit on the eggs at all times. Mama and Papa eagle take turns, but when it gets really cold they sit together on the eggs to keep them warm.

About 35 days after the eggs are laid, the eggs hatch and Mama and Papa have two beautiful baby eaglets. One is a girl and the other a boy. They decide to name them Scarlett and Liam.

For the next few weeks, the parents take turns sitting with Scarlett and Liam to keep them safe while the other parent hunts for food.

Mama and Papa bring all different kinds of food back to the nest: fish, snakes, rats and other small animals. Their favorite food is fish caught from the Hudson River.

Because eaglets Scarlett and Liam don't know how to break their own fish up, the parents feed them using their beaks.

On one sunny day while Papa stays in the nest with Scarlett and Liam, Mama sees a young bald eagle known as a juvenile. She feels that this other bird is a threat to her eaglets, so she chases it very far away.

After Mama chases the juvenile eagle away from her babies, she stands guard high in a pine tree to make sure that it does not return.

After 5 weeks of eating well, Scarlett and Liam get so big that the nest is too crowded to hold both eaglets and one of the parents, so Mama and Papa eagle leave the nest to sit on nearby branches. They continue to keep an eye on Scarlett and Liam, watching carefully to make sure that the babies are safe in the nest.

Then, one day in early spring, Scarlett decides it is time to leave the nest to check things out from a nearby branch. She still cannot fly, but she hops up and down, spreading her wings to see what they can do for her. This phase in an eaglet's life is referred to as branching.

The next day, Liam decides it is his turn to start branching. Now both eaglets are out of the nest and on branches.

As the days go by, Scarlett and Liam become braver and start to hop up onto higher branches. They spend hours looking around and stretching their wings to prepare for flight.

One sunny afternoon, about 11 weeks after the eaglets have hatched, Scarlett and Liam take flight. Now that they have taken flight they are no longer considered eaglets. They are now fledglings.

Through the remainder of the spring and summer, Scarlett and
Liam practice taking off, flying and landing in new areas.

They hang out on light posts, in trees and on rooftops. Even though they are learning to do all of these new and wonderful things, they stay close to the nest for safety.

The Mama and Papa eagles also stay very close to Scarlett and Liam and continue to bring them food because they have not yet learned how to get their own food. The parents do not want the fledglings to go back to the nest, so they deliver their food to locations farther and farther away.

One of the things Scarlett and Liam learn on this new journey is that other birds are not always nice to them. One day when Liam is sitting on the light post, a mockingbird starts body slamming into him. The mockingbird wants the light post all to himself.

Then, the very next day a mockingbird starts slamming into Scarlett and being really mean to her. Scarlett gets chased out of the tree by the little bird.

By the end of the summer Scarlett and Liam are so good at taking off, flying and landing that Mama and Papa lead them towards the Hudson River. It's time for the fledglings to learn how to catch their own fish.

Scarlett and Liam pay close attention as the Mama and Papa eagles show them how to fish. After lots of watching and practicing, Scarlett and Liam catch their own fish.

Now that Scarlett and Liam have left the nest and learned how to take care of themselves, the big nest in the tulip tree will stay empty until next winter when the Mama eagle lays new eggs and the Mama and Papa eagles raise a new family of eaglets.

The End

www.ingramcontent.com/pod-product-compliance
Lightning Source LLC
Chambersburg PA
CBHW060859270326
41935CB00003B/34